# THE NEW BOOK OF PATIENCE GAMES

Mystery, Mustery & Mastery
and some Jiggery-pokery

Ruth D. Botterill

## W. FOULSHAM & CO. LTD.
London · New York · Toronto · Cape Town · Sydney

# W. FOULSHAM & COMPANY LIMITED
*Yeovil Road, Slough, Berkshire SL1 4JH*

ISBN 0–572–01169–5

Printed in Great Britain by
St Edmundsbury Press, Bury St Edmunds, Suffolk

# CONTENTS

Smoke                        9
Move up                     10
Eight across                12
Jack be nimble              13
As you like                 15
Six fives                   17
Republic                    19
Tower of London             21
Equality                    24
Boxing Day                  25
Tournament                  28
Absorption                  30
Teaser                      31
Fanny                       33
Seek your own               35
Rapide or 12
    into 4                  36
Long nose                   38
Six sixes                   40
Foresight                   42
Match up                    44
Aces save                   45
Cover black                 47
Exchange                    49
Afternoon                   50
Chess-move                  52
Sevens & Sixes              54
Friday the 13th             56
Three tries                 58
The fives                   60
Recovery                    62

# INTRODUCTION

*'Happiness is absorption.'*

This is a book of Patience games for use with one pack of playing cards. To my knowledge all the games are original, but I should not be surprised if some of them have already been invented by keen players. I can only sincerely apologise if any readers find one or two games similar to ones they have themselves created.

The games are all designed with varying degrees of thought and time required to bring each to a satisfactory conclusion – in other words, to bring the cards into the desired order for that particular game. One or two are so quick that they can be played several times while the kettle boils. Others entail settling down for a long session; and what an excellent way to fill in time while 'playing a waiting game'!

As I have already mentioned, the Patience games in this book are each played with one pack of cards. The pack consists of four suits of cards: two black and two red, namely Clubs, Hearts, Spades and Diamonds. Each suit has cards numbered 1 (the Ace) to 10 and three court cards. The court cards are Kings, Queens and Jacks. Sometimes the Jack is called a Knave, but I have avoided that term lest it be confused with the King. The object of many Patience games is to build up the four suits on their respective Aces. To that end the Aces are removed to the side, either before play begins or as they become exposed during play. (An exposed card is one that is not overlapped by another.) When, during play, the cards are built up in suits on the Aces, the cards are laid on top of each other and do not overlap.

Playing Patience (also known as Solitaire) should not be regarded with scorn or hauteur, for heads of state and other wielders of power have realised its therapeutic value. But it should not be regarded as a therapy only, or a treatment for jangling nerves. The games are a pleasure in themselves. In fact, we only play for pleasure. Whatever other benefits we may derive, we really only play for the pleasure of the games.

4

There is always the thrill of the pack as you pick it up and shuffle it, not knowing the order in which the cards will come up, but knowing that the whole game depends upon that order. The word 'order' is ambiguous, meaning in fact two opposite conditions. The cards you pick up are not actually *in order*, unless by a million-to-one chance you have shuffled them into a set pattern. Often little patterns will appear, such as the four Aces turning up together, but usually your pack, when you begin to play is 'at random', and out of that disorder you will contrive, move by move, to bring about the satisfaction of order, and with it contentment.

Nearly all the games in this book begin with a set pattern. A few keep the same shape until nearly the end of the game, but usually the pattern begins to change as the game proceeds. In three instances there is no regular formation to begin with. For each game, there is an illustration showing how it is laid out, and another which shows the game at a later stage of play.

The games differ in the demands they make on the player. Some are wholly mechanical, requiring only the playing to the rules; depending on the order of the cards there can be only one result. Others present different courses of action, the outcome depending upon what choices are made, though there is very little strain on the brain. Some require foresight and intelligence, thinking in a number of directions at the same time, and the ability to compare mentally various moves, and foresee the results, planning a number of moves ahead. Some games cannot go out if play is blocked. Some will always go out if the right moves are made. Sometimes an impasse can be prevented or relieved by the exercise of an option. There is usually some choice here. In order to add further interest, I played each game twenty times in succession, recording the results which, in some cases, surprised me. You will find the results relevant to each game in a footnote following the instructions. Do not be unduly influenced by these statistics, however, for I may have exercised less skill than you will and, who knows, the Moon may not always have been in the right quarter for winning!

I started this preamble with a quotation, whose source I

can no longer find. To turn the quotation round, absorption is happiness. It doesn't matter how deeply you are involved in 'unpleasantries', if you become absorbed in watching, listening, or, particularly, doing something, you forget. Your negative thoughts have floated away. Here I offer you the chance to become absorbed.

Some games are especially therapeutic, as we play out our frustrations through the cards. In real life we may feel helpless or incompetent, bored or overworked, our minds unstretched or stretched too far. Here are games that give us a chance to play out our dissatisfactions in complete absorption, in addition to being entertaining, relaxing or exhilarating.

You can play Patience almost anywhere, (from a cellar to a summerhouse, from a station to a bivouac), though some places are more convenient than others. The amount of space needed varies with different games. There are, however, more comfortable ways to play. You will need a flat surface. It is easier if your table is not shiny or covered with a moveable cloth. The shifting about of the cards can be frustrating. Small Patience cards are best, if you can manipulate them comfortably. They take up less space, and it is easier to see the whole spread of the cards.

When a friend of mine was unfortunately deprived of the use of her right arm, she found with delight that she could play Patience using her left hand. She could shuffle the cards by shaking them out on the table face-down, and then describing a figure-of-eight with her fingertips, mixing them thoroughly. After shuffling she bunched them together with her hand and neatened them. She could then pick up one card at a time, and so the games began. You will find in the Index which games she could play.

Deafness is no obstacle to the games, either; in fact it is almost an asset, as you are not likely to be disturbed by a call to do a job, or to take part in that extraordinary activity known as stretching the legs. Ever since childhood people have, now and again, urged me to 'Get out and stretch your legs. It will do you good.' The abandonment of a comfortable position in which I am contentedly settled has always seemed quite unnecessary, and as for the promised beneficial effects, I have always found them to be grossly overrated. A good memory is useful but not a bit necessary.

How you feel about the finish of a game depends upon your attitude to it. You know that with every game, except a few certainties, it may or may not go out. There is always a degree of disappointment when play is blocked, but although it is satisfying to experience the minor triumph of a 'win', the fact that things do not always work out is both exasperating and fascinating. To some people the actual winning is of such vital importance that they are prepared to do a little surreptitious cheating to attain that end. For others 'the game's the thing', be the end what it may, and to these latter people, bending the rules holds no attractions.

That brings me to the subject of Jiggery-pokery. I have used this term to mean moving the cards in ways that are not included in the actual rules for that game, but that are not actually 'illegal'. Thus, in any game, exposed cards may be brought back from the suit sets to be used again in play if by so doing the game can be kept going when it would otherwise be blocked. (A card is said to be exposed when it is face-up and no other card is covering or overlapping it.) In one or two games another form of Jiggery-pokery can be employed.

One benefit of knowing a number of different games is that if one game continues to be awkward in refusing to work out you can switch to another.

It is a matter of your attitude to the game (according to your personality) whether you go right to the end. If you get to the stage where it is obvious that all blockages are freed and there is nothing to stop your progress towards the intended conclusion, you may enjoy putting all the remaining cards into their sets. Or is the realisation that the game will move to a satisfactory conclusion enough in itself, without actually moving the cards?

Each game starts with its own individual pattern. Only two start with identical lays. If you like to go from one game to another you will find that in some cases the order of the cards at the finish of one is such that another game can be immediately and easily laid. So the end of one can be the beginning of another.

How differently people view things! The paintings hanging on the walls of my house often prove a talking point, and it intrigues me to hear a visitor express a preference for one of them. I wonder why he likes that one better than the others. Different people like different pictures. It is the same with these games. We each have our favourites, and there are plenty to choose from. Some we may try a few times and then not play again for a long time, perhaps for ever. Some we play over and over again. I have found, though, that if I have not played a certain game for some time, when I go back to it new subtleties have sometimes been revealed which escaped me before.

Now, why the sub-title to each game? Before you begin any of the games you pick up the complete pack of cards. You shuffle them and then stop, ready to begin the first lay-out (or lay, as I shall call it.) There in your hand is the Mystery. You do not know, you cannot guess, how the cards will appear as you deal them one by one. Each has its own significance as it is revealed in its turn, and together they form a set pattern of bizarre and unordered significance. Even after the first action is completed there is in many cases the continuing Mystery of the unrevealed cards. In two games all the cards are both revealed and exposed. In several others all the cards are on view but only some are exposed. In the majority of cases some of the Mystery persists until nearly the end of the game.

When you have surveyed the cards after the first lay, you at once begin to plot your course of action. In many cases it is clear that you have no choice. You must move certain cards in a certain way. These actions you are obliged to take, and herein is the Mustery. There is, in some games, so little choice that they are almost entirely Mustery to the end.

After the Mystery and the Mustery comes the Mastery, when you really pit your wits against the situation, and everything depends upon the choices you make. Under the title of each game is indicated which of the three are involved in the playing of that game. So – Mystery, Mustery and Mastery are here for your delight.

# SMOKE

*Mystery, Mustery, Mastery*

Lay out nine cards in a row from left to right, face-up. The rest of the cards are the face-down feed-pack. Build any one of the nine cards on any other that you can in descending order and alternate colours, slightly overlapping. Only one card may be moved at any one time. In other words, cards placed on each other cannot be moved together onto another row. Take out any exposed Aces, place them at the bottom on your right to build on them upwards in suits, as the cards in sequence become exposed. When no more building is possible, put a card from the top of the feed-pack in each and every available space in the original row. Continue all possible building, one card at a time. Repeat filling the spaces and building as before.

When there are no spaces, lay a card from the feed-pack overlapping on each and every *single* card in the row to make twos, then continue building. Every time you have completed all possible building, lay cards from the feed-pack one at a time on all the *smallest* sets of cards in the row, – that is, to fill gaps, *or* to make single cards into twos, or twos into threes, and so on – completing the row each time before starting to build again. Continue the laying and building until the feed-pack is exhausted. At this stage (but not before), if a space can be manoeuvred in the original row, it may be filled by any card that is exposed. The game is completed when, and if, the four suits have been built up on their respective Aces.

*Went out  8*
      *20*

This was the first game I invented and it is still one of my favourites. The game is all Mustery until the whole pack is laid, when some legitimate Jiggery-pokery may enable necessary cards to be freed for building. If a space can be made in

Ready to start

In progress

the nine lay-out places by moving cards one at a time from one set to another (keeping in sequence) any exposed card can be put in the space and there is hope that the game can be completed.

# MOVE UP

*Mystery, Mustery, Mastery*

*Action 1* Lay a row of five cards face up, and another similar row beneath the first row. The rest of the cards are the feed-pack. Take out any exposed Aces and put them to the right for building up in suits later. Any suitable card in the rows can now be used to cover completely any other card in descending order and alternate colours, moving only one card at a time. When no further card will fit, move up each card or built-up pack in the bottom row directly on top of the card, cards or space above. Lay out another five cards to form another bottom row. Build up as before then move the bottom cards up as before. Play in this way until all the cards in the feed-pack are used.

*Action 2*  Pick up the heaps in order from the left into a pack, and without shuffling, turn the cards over. This is again the feed-pack. Lay the first card face down at the left side, to indicate the second deal. Repeat the process as in *Action 1*, finishing by turning over the card at the left, and using it as you would the last card in the feed-pack.

*Action 3*  Pick up the heaps in any order you please for the third and final deal. Play as in *Action 1* until all the suits are built up or no further move is possible.

*Went out  8*
            *20*

---

This is a neat game which does not sprawl in any direction. All building is done directly on top of other cards and there is no overlapping. Play is simple and straightforward for the first two actions. When you come to the end of *Action 2*, the heaps in the rows will contain mixed sequences. Since the higher-value cards will not be required until the end of the game, and since they will block play if they appear too soon, you will need to pick up the heaps that contain most court card sequences first so that they will then be paid out last.

As a variation, begin with two rows of four cards.

Ready to start          In progress

# EIGHT ACROSS

## Mystery, Mastery

Lay four cards in a downward line at the left face-up. Lay another four cards similarly at the right with a space between the lines. This space should be the width of six cards. If any two of these eight cards are of similar number, move one alongside its twin, between the rows. That twin has now 'progressed'. Make as many progressions as possible, forming triplets and eventually quads.

When no more progressions can be made, lay a further card from the feed-pack on top of every card (and space) in the original two rows that has not progressed. Carry out any more progressing that can be done, using the exposed cards only, then continue with a further lay as before until all cards in the feed-pack are used and all possible progressions have been made. The object is to obtain four full rows of eight. When there are three and a half rows complete, the cards in the hand may be fanned, face-up, and extractions made to fit the last unprogressed card.

| | | |
|---|---|---|
| Score of 4  1 | Score of 2  6 | Score of 0  2 |
| 36 | 20 | 20 |
| Score of 3  2 | Score of 1  10 | |
| 20 | 20 | |

---

Here is a quick game which occasionally gets home, and many times gets very nearly there. A score of four is the ultimate. The earlier the progressing starts, the more likelihood there is that the eights will be completed. As each lay is made, further matching cards may appear which can add to the progressions. If you lay two cards that match, and you know that another card of that number is covered and unlikely to become exposed, it is obviously no use making them into a progression, so they should be left unmatched,

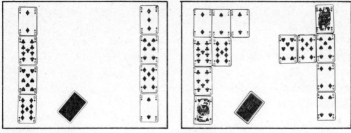

Ready to start · In progress

and covered as usual by the next lay. Whenever a card is to be used for twinning, it is judicious to look below each of the twins to see which card is the more likely to be useful for making another progression.

# JACK BE NIMBLE

*Mystery, Mustery*

Lay the four Jacks face-up in a downward diagonal row, corner to corner, in the order: Clubs – Hearts – Spades – Diamonds. Shuffle the rest of the cards. From this face-down feed-pack lay (face-up) one card below the Jack of Clubs, one below the Jack of Hearts, one below the Jack of Spades, one above the Jack of Hearts, one above the Jack of Spades and one above the Jack of Diamonds. It is as well to consult the diagram where these six placings are numbered 1 to 6. A Jack may now jump over any adjacent card of the same suit as himself, up, down or sideways, but not diagonally, and any cards so jumped over are removed to their own corner – Clubs to the top left corner of the board, Hearts to the top right, Spades to the bottom left corner, and Diamonds to the bottom right corner. As in the game of draughts the Jack may take as many cards as become adjacent in one move. Replace each taken card with the top card of the feed-pack.

When no further move is possible lay six more cards from the feed-pack in the places 1 to 6, covering any already there.

The Jack now jumps as before, but takes only the top card of any heap he jumps over. A replacement card is only added if a place becomes vacant. One Jack may land on top of another. Only the top Jack may then move when an opportunity arises. Keep taking where possible, then add six further cards as before until the four suits are complete or no further move is possible.

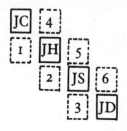

*Went out*  0
          20

*1 game, only 2 cards left.*

---

The odds against this game going out are very long indeed. Nevertheless there is always the knowledge that it *could* go out, and there is always hope. The pattern of the six non-Jack cards must be memorised, and a clear head kept to avoid confusion when laying each subsequent six cards, and even when placing the single replacements, as it is easy to put a card in the wrong place. However, once the pattern is learnt, each game played makes it easier to remember. It is a quick game, once you have found the Jacks!

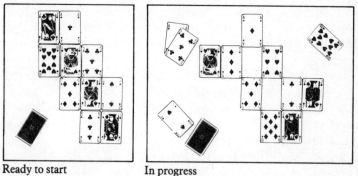

Ready to start       In progress

# AS YOU LIKE

## Mystery, Mastery

*Action 1*   Hold the pack face-down. Take four cards from the top and lay them in a stack on the table face-up. Take another four from the pack. If the exposed card of the second four is the same colour as the top card of the first four, lay the second group on top of the first one. If it is different start another stack. Keep taking fours, matching black or red on the two stacks until the pack is exhausted.

*Action 2*   Pick up one of the two newly-formed packs, black or red as you like, turn the cards over and lay them from left to right in separate rows of four, each row downward and overlapping with only the fourth card face-up.

*Action 3*   Pick up and turn over the second pack. Take the cards four at a time and put them face-up in a heap. Use the exposed card of this heap to build on any card in the rows, in descending order and alternate colour. When the top card is so used, any newly exposed card may now be used to build. Any exposed card or building can be moved to build onto another card or building. Remove Aces to the side and build on them upwards in suits. When a King is exposed he may fill any space that has been formed by the removal of a row. If there is no space the King is put in a courtesy place at the bottom left of the table, to wait until a space occurs. Any King waiting in the courtesy place may be built on from the discard pack or the rows, but not overlapping, in descending and alternate order, but until he is moved with his followers into a space he has no privileges, in other words he may not receive more than one card at a time. When a space occurs his whole building may be moved from the courtesy place and put in the space, overlapping like the other rows, and more than one card at a time may then be added to his building. Continue to deal the feed-pack in fours, (there may be less than four cards at the end of the deal) and each time it becomes exhausted turn the heap for re-use until no further move can be made.

Ready to start

In progress

*Action 4* Continue as before, but deal the feed-pack in groups of three cards. The game is won when all the four suits are built up.

*Went out 10*
    *20*

One of the fascinations of this game is the variability of the starting position. After the preliminary action which divides the pack into two parts you may find one part much larger than the other. Then you must choose which is the better selection – to lay the larger pack or the smaller one. It would take a mathematician to evaluate the odds one way or the other. One deciding factor is the knowledge that with the pack in your hand you will have eventually the saving change of deal from four to three cards at a time. Of course there is the possibility that after the first dividing you will be left with only one set of four in one pack. What are the odds then? It seems that the large pack had better be laid. But is that really so? It is an intriguing question. There is also the possibility that all the exposed cards in the first division will be of the same colour. In that case you will not have to choose at all!

In Patience, Kings are encountered with mixed feelings. There is triumph when they arrive expediently at the right time to put the finishing touch to the game, or they can turn up at just the wrong moment and indeed often sabotage the whole affair, causing an inevitable breakdown. In this game the Kings would certainly block further action if there were not a courtesy place to which they can be conducted with suitable dignity, where their sovereignty is not impaired, and where they can wait patiently for their chance to be re-instated.

# SIX FIVES

### *Mystery, Mustery, Mastery*

*Action 1*   Lay six packs of five cards in a row from left to right face down. Turn the six top cards face-up. Put the remaining twenty-two cards in a feed-pack face-down. Place any possible exposed card on top of one of the next highest rank, regardless of colour or suit, turning over the face-down card thus revealed, which can now be used as an exposed card for building onto another suitable exposed card or Ace. Place Aces below, and build up in suits. If a place becomes vacant replace with the top card of the feed-pack, and build as before.

*Action 2*   After the first set of moves, when no further card can be played, move all the face-up cards one place down in

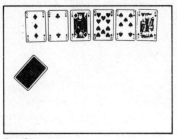

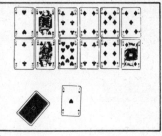

Ready to start                                    In progress

their built-up sets, filling any spaces so created with a card
from the feed-pack. Turn up the top cards of the face-down
packs and repeat the building on the twelve places, filling the
gaps as before, and complete the suits being built on the
Aces. If at the end any King is left exposed on top of a
face-down pack that King may be moved down on its own
and the next card turned face-up. Repeat the process until no
more moves can be made. The object of the game is to
complete the four suits from the exposed cards.

*Went out 10*
    *20*

In this game there is much movement of cards from one heap
to another. If you have a choice, when transferring one, put
it, if possible, onto the card of its own suit so that when the
top card is taken for building on its own Ace, further cards
are available in the same suit.

When you seem to have come to a full-stop, where no card
is available for play, a little Jiggery-pokery can sometimes
save the day. You can transfer cards (one at a time) from one
building to others, thus whittling down the first building and
creating a space, or revealing a face-down card which can
then be turned. Such actions may expose a required card, and
so the game gets a new lease of life. It is also possible, by the
same Jiggery-pokery, to reveal cards which are needed for
building up the suits on the Aces. If, for example, you need
the 4 of Hearts, and the 3 of Diamonds is at the top of one
building and the 4 of Spades on another, by transferring the 3
to the 4 you may find the 4 of Hearts now exposed.

# REPUBLIC

## Mastery

*Action 1*  Lay eight cards in a downwards row face-up and overlapping. This can be understood as one card and seven followers. Lay four more similar rows alongside. Put the remaining twelve cards in a pack, face-down, as a reserve. The object of the game is to build down in suits from 10 to Ace. As each 10 is exposed it is placed to the right of the rows. These are covered by the 9s, as they become exposed, and so on down to the Aces. To expose a required card, the one overlapping it is moved onto an exposed card of similar number to itself, taking with it any followers, regardless of what the followers are. By judicious moves, one or more 10s can become available, and then the other numbers in order made available likewise.

As a picture card is exposed it is removed to a discard heap and replaced by the card at the top of the reserve. Before this replacement is made, any required manoeuvres may be done. The replacement card is then placed, always being laid on the row from which the court card was removed. A King may move to a space together with his followers, but when exposed he must be removed and replaced. If a court card is turned up in the hand as a replacement, remove it and use the next card. As the court cards are removed, put them in a face-down heap at the side, except for the Kings. Place the four Kings, as they are removed in turn, in a separate heap face-up.

*Action 2*  This move may only be made if the reserve is used up. (If it is not used up and no further moves can be made the game is lost.) Once only, pick up all the cards in the rows, and the four Kings. Shuffle them. Lay five cards in a face-up row from left to right. Lay the next five cards in a similar row below, overlapping the first row. Continue laying the cards in rows of five until the pack is exhausted. There is no replacing in this action. A King may still move into a space with his followers, but is removed if exposed. Continue as in

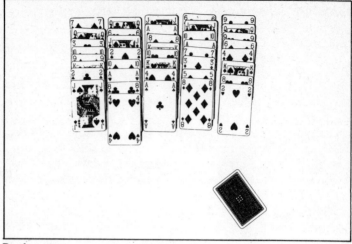

Ready to start

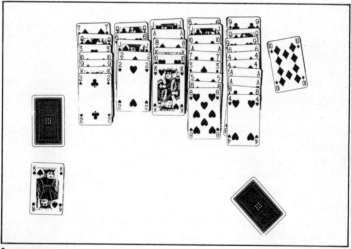

In progress

*Action 1*, building on the 10s until all the Aces have been placed.

*Went out* 9
          20

There is an unusual method of building in this game. In the majority of games a set of cards overlapping downwards may only be removed *en bloc* if they are in a descending sequence, but in this game unrelated sets of cards are moved together, depending only on the number of the card at the beginning of the set. It is a game requiring a lot of Mastery and usually takes time. It will nearly always go out if the right moves are made, but there are pitfalls to be avoided. If the suits cannot be completed in *Action 1* it is imperative to dispense with all the picture cards. This is impossible if a set of four of the same number directly covers a picture card, so this must be avoided. A set of four always blocks the covered card unless the four can be used for building the suits. In the second lay it is fatal to get a set of four over a card of higher denomination. The game is then dead. The use of the King to take his followers into a space can sometimes save the day, either in the first or second lay. If all four cards of one number are in the same row with a card or cards between, it is sometimes impossible to move them. If the separating cards are court cards the game is lost except in two cases. A King can take his following cards to a space enabling the set of four to be manoeuvred. Then again, the complete set of four may be the four required for building suits, and so they and the required cards can be released.

If all the 10s, then all the 9s and so on, can be exposed and built it sometimes works out better than continuing to build on one suit at a time.

# TOWER OF LONDON

*Mystery, Mustery, Mastery*

Place the King, then the Queen, then the Jack of Clubs face-up in a downward row at the left, slightly overlapping. Do the same with each set of court cards, making four rows of three, but leaving a space between each suit and the next. These royal persons are 'in prison', so to guard them place four cards downwards overlapping between each two suits,

Ready to start

In progress

and four at each side. Put one card below each set of three royal cards. Thus the royal groups are all guarded on three sides. Put the remaining sixteen cards in a face-down heap. They become the feed-pack. The King can build up his bodyguard on the fourth side, in other words above his head.

Start the game by using the exposed cards to build downwards in descending order and alternate colours. Any such building may be removed as a whole for building onto another exposed card. As an Ace is exposed, place it above its respective King and build on it in order up to 10. However, before the 10 is reached the royal prisoners may have escaped. When a space occurs below a Jack that Jack escapes, and is placed below and away from the general lay-out. Since the guard was not strong enough put two cards from the feed-pack below the Queen. Continue to build. A space below the Queen allows that Queen to escape and so two more cards must be put below the King. If a space occurs in a row beside the prisoners any exposed 10 or a 10 with a built-up sequence may be put in the space. When all twelve prisoners have escaped the game is finished.

*All escaped* 7
    20

---

Four Kings, four Queens and four Jacks imprisoned in the Tower of London. In reality they would probably have not escaped, but here we can work out a fantasy in which we ourselves are able to effect their escape, or at least to do our utmost to achieve that end. It is a triumph if all the prisoners escape, and if they don't we can sweep the cards together knowing that it was only a fantasy after all.

The Jack has one card below to guard him. If he escapes, a stronger guard must be mounted, and two cards are placed to guard the Queen. If she also escapes, two more cards must guard the King. When an Ace becomes free it is placed above the King's head, this time to protect him, and his own suit is built up with reinforcements until he, too, can escape. There is no need to build up the suits if all the prisoners escape, for that is the end of the game.

# EQUALITY

## *Mystery, Mustery*

Lay ten cards from the top of the pack face-down in a heap at the top – 12 o'clock. Lay another similar ten cards at each side – 9 o'clock and 3 o'clock. Turn over the top card of each heap of ten. If any two cards thus exposed are of the same number remove them both to a throwaway heap at the side and turn over the next face-down cards. Whether you have matched any cards or not, turn over one card from the feed-pack. If this card is the same number as any of the three exposed cards remove these two matching cards to the throwaway heap and turn up the top face-down card of the heap from which the matching card was removed. If not, continue by turning over the top cards of the feed-pack one at a time. Match and remove any two exposed cards, including any from the feed-pack that matches one just played. The feed-pack is turned over and played again and again. Continue until all the cards in the feed-pack are exhausted or no further match is possible.

| All pairs | 1 | 25 pairs | 1 | Nearly all pairs | 6 |
|---|---|---|---|---|---|
| | 20 | | 20 | | 20 |

---

Here is a very simple game requiring no effort of thought. It sometimes goes out.

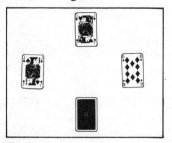

Ready to start

In progress

# BOXING DAY

*Mystery, Mustery, Mastery*

*Action 1* Lay a card face-up on the left. Lay six more cards to the right of the first one, alternately face-up and face-down, making a row of seven. Immediately beneath them lay a similar row of seven cards, alternating with each other and with the ones above. The rest of the cards are the face-down feed-pack. Aces are taken out as they appear and built on to complete the suits. Start the game by taking any exposed card that can be built onto another of one higher denomination, irrespective of colour or suit, and place it on top of that card. Its place is then filled by the top card of the feed-pack. At the same time the next card from the feed-pack is placed face-down on top of the face-down card below or above the replaced face-up card. Continue to build downwards in this way and replace two cards each time. When no further exposed card can be used for building (only one exposed card at a time may move), lay one card from the feed-pack face-up on top of each exposed card. Continue building and laying cards, and building up on the Aces, until all the pack is used.

*Action 2* Pick up in order all the face-down cards into a face-down feed-pack. Fan out all the face-up heaps, except the suits on the Aces. Turn up one card from the feed-pack and place it face-up at the bottom of the table, unless you are able to add it to a fan. You may add it to any fan where it will fit in descending order. Continue to turn the feed-pack one card at a time. If you cannot build with a card, place it at the bottom and any others that cannot be built should be overlapped sideways. Build up on the Aces from both the exposed cards in the fans and by the exposed card from the feed-pack. Each exposed card can be used to build as before, including the card exposed at the top of the discard-fan. Any King that becomes exposed may at your discretion be removed to the bottom of the heap on which he appeared. The feed-pack in

Ready to start

In progress

*Action 2* may only be used once. Continue building until all the suits are complete, or until no further move is possible.

*Went out 12*
     *20*

At first this game seems self-destroying, but further tries reveal the subtleties of Jiggery-pokery which can often save the day. In fact, the game is almost entirely Jiggery-pokery, and its fascination lies in the switching about of the cards. Because the laying of seven further cards on the exposed cards often blocks the later play it is best to prevent, for as long as possible, the necessity for such an action. At times it

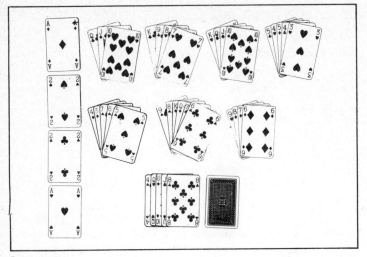

Later stage

cannot be avoided, but often you will be able to continue to remove a card to another heap and replace it with one other. Sometimes when you remove the top, exposed card from a heap, you will find that the card now exposed can also be used. You may remove that card and any other that becomes exposed in that heap before you put on the replacement card. However many cards are removed from one heap at a time, only one card from the feed-pack is placed on top, and only one other on the adjacent face-down heap. A card that is already built can be moved onto another suitable card. This can minimise blockages. (It is as well to build the highest card possible every time and progress to lower ones.)

After the face-down cards have been picked up, and the paying-out one by one of this feed-pack begins, it will be seen that further Jiggery-pokery can be done. In order that the cards now being dealt do not become irretrievably blocked, the cards already exposed (including those built in suits) can be moved, one at a time, to other fans, thus often providing an opening for the card exposed on the feed-pack fan, or freeing a necessary card from another fan.

# TOURNAMENT

## Mystery, Mastery

Lay four cards side by side face-up towards the top at the left. Lay three more cards below, overlapping slightly the spaces of the four above. Lay two similarly below, and then one below them, to complete the pattern. Lay another set in the same way to the right of the first set. Just below, place one card in the centre. Lay two cards slightly below and overlapping this card. Lay three and then four cards so that this pattern is the reverse of the patterns above. The remainder of the cards become the face-down feed-pack. Any exposed (not overlapped) card may be played to build downwards on any other exposed card in a descending order regardless of colour or suit, and regardless of which set it belongs to. Any set so made or part of a set may be moved for such building. If any of the cards in a top row become exposed do not remove them except to build on Aces.

The Aces, when they become exposed, are removed and placed above the top rows, red on the right and black on the left. Build on them upwards in suits as cards become exposed. Kings and Queens when exposed may be removed to the side, red royalty to the right and black to the left. They are placed sideways, the Queen on the King's right. If thought expedient the Kings and Queens can remain and take part in the game. The Jacks have three options. You may remove them to the side as with the Kings and Queens, you may leave them in play, or they may be placed at the top, each next to his own Ace, to be available for play towards the end of the game. When no further moves can be made – when all possible building has been done – deal the feed-pack in threes into a face-up heap, the top card of the three thus becoming exposed and available for use in building as above. If this card is played the exposed card below can be used to build on the exposed cards or buildings; similarly any card in the heap which becomes exposed. Every time the feed-pack is

Ready to start

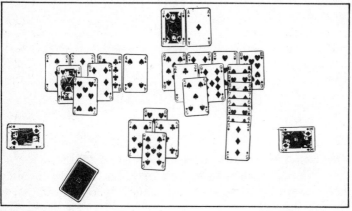

In progress

exhausted pick up the discard heap, turn it and deal it again in threes. Continue building until the suits are complete to the 10.

If, before the suits are completed, no further move can be made, any Jack may be brought down from the top (though not from the side) of the table, and placed on his own side of the first row of cards laid; in other words black on the left and red on the right. The 10 of that suit, together with any cards built on it, can then be moved onto the Jack, thus releasing other cards for play. The 10 thus moved must be of the same suit as the Jack.

Now, here's a bit of make-believe to add zest to the game. The table is the field with galleries at the sides where the royalty may sit and watch the contest, or they may join in if they feel so inclined. The Jacks are the marshals who, as they become free, may wait at the top of the field, each next to his own Ace. The game can usually, but not always, be brought to a satisfactory conclusion, with all the suits built up to the Jack, and the Queens and Kings can join their own suits. It may be that the King will congratulate the marshal if by his timely intervention he has saved the day by preventing a breakdown of the games.

# ABSORPTION

*Mystery, Mastery*

Lay nine cards in a row from left to right face-up. The rest of the cards are the face-down feed-pack. Put any card or cards from the original nine that match another in number below and overlapping that one. When no more can be matched, lay another row of nine cards below and overlapping those already laid and including any space. Place one or more matching cards overlapping similar numbers as before. Continue thus, dealing the remaining cards nine at a time and building sets of four of each denomination until the pack is used. As soon as a set of four similar cards is completed remove it to the side. When no further move is possible count the full sets for your score.

*All 4s complete  5*
20                          *Average no. of 4s 7½*

There is considerable choice of action here. In moving one

Ready to start

In progress

card or set of cards to another, make a judicious choice depending on the card which will become exposed, for you will find that it is possible to plot a number of moves before moving any cards. It does not often happen that the whole 13 sets are made up, but the more sets you can get the more satisfying is the game.

# TEASER

*Mastery*

Sort the pack into sets, putting the four Aces together, the four 2s and so on. Discard the Jacks. Pick up the cards in order as follows: Kings first, then 10s, 9s, 8s and so on to Aces, and last of all the Queens. Lay the cards, as they come, face-up in the following manner: put the four Queens on the left in a downward row. To the right of them put the Aces, then the 2s and so on, finishing with the Kings, to complete twelve rows of four cards, or four rows of twelve cards. Rearrange the Kings so that the Queen is of the same suit as the King in each row. In order to obtain a complete suit of all cards in each row exchange any card with the one immediately below it, but only when one of these cards is directly between two cards of the same suit *as each other*. The royal cards do not move, but the suit of each is of consequence when you wish to move a card next to it, in other words, a 10 or an Ace.

*Went out 20*
     *20*

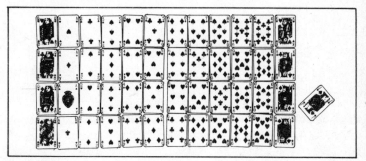

Ready to start

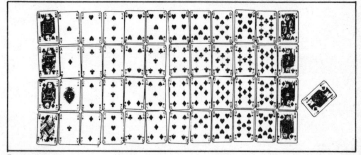

In progress

This teasing game has an affinity with the Chinese puzzles in which tiny numbered tiles are moved one at a time to achieve a given order. No doubt one could spend a lifetime trying to reach that desired end without ever getting there. This game is, fortunately, neither so long nor so frustrating, and putting the last card in place is something to smile about.

# FANNY

## *Mystery, Mustery, Mastery*

*Action 1* Hold the pack face-up and take off the cards in twos. Separate each pair by putting the higher card to the right and the lower to the left, making two heaps. (N.B. Ace is low, King is high.) If you turn up two cards of the same number put them in a heap at the top, away from the other two heaps. Continue dividing the cards thus until the pack is finished. You now have two half-packs at the bottom. Push the right-hand pack further away.

*Action 2* Pick up the left-hand heap and divide it exactly as in *Action 1*. If there is an odd card left over, add it to the half-pack at the far right. You now have two quarter-packs near you. Push the right-hand quarter-pack a little further to the right.

*Action 3* Pick up the left-hand heap and divide it as in *Action 1*, adding any odd card to the right-hand quarter-heap. You now have two eighth-packs. Fan each eighth-pack, without altering the order of the cards. (To fan the cards spread them in a fan shape so that they are overlapping with just the corner denominations and suits visible, except for the top – exposed – card which is completely visible.)

*Action 4* Pick up the right-hand quarter-pack and divide it as in *Action 3*. Fan the resulting packs.

*Action 5* Repeat *Actions 1–4* with the right-hand half-pack. You now have eight fans at the bottom, and a heap of twins at the top.

Ready to start          In progress

*Action 6*   Bring down the twins and make them into a fan (in this instance we shall call it a twin-fan). The order of the cards in the twin-fan is of no significance. Any card in this fan may be used at any time, regardless of its place in the fan.

*Action 7*   Pick up any one fan, with the exception of the twin-fan, which will satisfy the following requirement: each and every card in the fan must be next in number to, and the same suit as, one or more exposed cards on the other fans, and/or a card or cards in its own fan, and/or a card or cards in the twin-fan. (N.B. The Ace is next to the King, as well as to the 2.) Put these cards in overlapping lines at the top of the table, each suit in a row of its own. No card in the chosen fan must be left unused. Now find another fan that can be used in the same way and repeat the process. (After the first fans have been laid in the suit-lines, single cards from the picked-up fan may be added to any such built line, in the required sequence.) Continue in this way until all the cards are built in the four suit-lines, or no further fan can be used.

*Went out 15*
    *20*

---

At the beginning of *Action* 7 you may find that only one fan can be used, but as the game progresses more fans usually become suitable for use. When considering the suitability of a fan, bear in mind that the order in which you play the cards is important. By removing a certain exposed card from another fan, a further card will become exposed, which is available for use immediately. Build as many cards as possible each time.

This game is all fans, and ends (if it does) with fanned lines of the complete four suits.


# SEEK YOUR OWN

*Mystery, Mustery*


Lay thirteen cards in a downward row face-up, each overlapping the one above. If any card is of the same denomination as another, move the one and slip it in above or below the other. Take the face-down pack that is left and turn up a set of three. Place this set of three in a heap. If the exposed card matches one or more in the downward row slip it in as before. Do the same with the card now showing if it will fit. When the exposed card will not fit anywhere turn up another three and place this set on top of the first turned-up cards, then match as before if possible. Continue through the feed-pack, then turn it over and repeat turning sets of three until no further exposed card can be placed. As each set of four cards is completed remove the set. Continue using the feed-pack for turning and matching until the sets are complete, or no further card can be matched.

| *All cards removed in 4s* | 2 | *Average score 6* |
|---|---|---|
| | 20 | 9 |

It is not often that the fours are all made up, and the original line is completely removed. There is no fixed number of the sets of four. The maximum would be thirteen.

When dealing the threes it becomes obvious that some will never become broken up. If the exposed card on the first turn-up does not match any in the original line, the complete

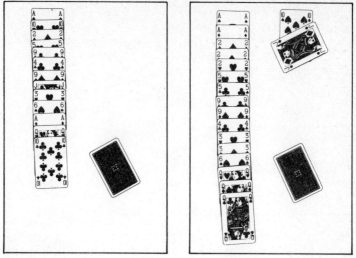

Ready to start      In progress

three cards can be set aside, because the same card is always going to be the exposed one of that three, and the two cards below it are blocked from use. Try the next three cards, and if the exposed one will not go, that three can be discarded also. Continue in this way until a turn-up of three reveals a card that will match. The removal of this card means that the two cards below can be left in play, and the pack can continue to be dealt. The position of the cards with further turns will vary as exposed matching cards are removed.

# RAPIDE OR 12 INTO 4

*Mystery, Mastery*

Lay the first twelve cards from the pack face up in three rows of four. Put any exposed card on top of another if that card is next to, or next but one to, it in numerical order (either

Ready to start                    In progress

higher or lower) and of the same suit. Thus the Queen of Hearts can be placed on top of the 10, Jack, King or Ace of Hearts. As a space occurs fill it with the top card of the pack. As little heaps are formed move the whole heap when the top, exposed, card is to be placed on another card or heap as described above. The game finishes when no further cards can be moved, or the pack is exhausted. The game 'goes out' when four heaps are formed with one complete suit in each.

*4 heaps completed   0*             *5 heaps completed   2*
             20                                 20

---

This is indeed a quick game. It rarely goes out, but is intriguing in the different systems that can be employed, each of which might 'succeed this time'. The moveable cards can be played as they appear, in a haphazard way, or you can build up or down to a chosen number so that the game should finish with four heaps topped with, say, four Kings, or four 7s, or whatever number you choose. Or you can concentrate on, say, the blacks, leaving the reds until no further blacks can be moved, then switching to the reds. This is a game in which the head often moves faster than the hand.

A reasonable system is to build towards a card that does not yet match. The exposed cards of one suit might be 2, 6 and 8. You could put the 6 on the 8, thus building towards the 2. It is as well to replace each card immediately, rather than do a number of moves and then make replacements.

# LONG NOSE

## *Mystery, Mustery*

Place four cards face-up in a downward row in the centre.
Place another similar row alongside. A little to the left place
eight cards in an overlapping ring face-up. Place a similar
circle on the right. Put the remaining cards face-down in a
feed-pack. The centre cards form the beginnings of buildings. This building is done sideways, and always away from
the centre. The left-hand row is built on in downward
sequence and the right-hand row progresses in upward sequence, always in the same suit. Thus an Ace in the left-hand
row progresses through the King and Queen down to the 2,
and an Ace in the right row progresses upwards through the 2
and the 3 to the King. Whatever cards are in the centre rows
are built on in similar order.

The object of the game is to complete all four suits using
the rows in the centre. When any card in either of the rings
will fit on any one of the centre cards at the left, as described
above, remove it and slip it under that card so that the
number is just visible. If any card fits onto a right-hand card
place it over that card, slightly overlapping. Progression may
only be made to the right in the right-hand row and to the left

Ready to start

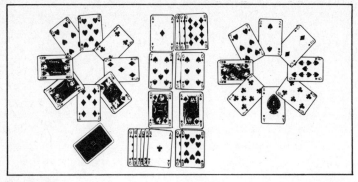

In progress

in the left-hand row. As a space occurs in a ring or in a centre row fill it with the top card of the feed-pack. Any fitting progression may be removed from the right row and slipped under a card or progression on the left. Similarly, a fitting left-hand card or progression may be placed on top of a right-hand card or progression. The game ends when the four suit progressions are complete, or no further card can be played.

*Went out* 7
    20

A long nose and two eyes. A nice pattern to start with. It would seem that with twenty-four cards, in other words nearly half the pack, exposed, the game is almost certain to go out, but this is not so. Many a game reaches the point where, of the eight cards required for building, not one is exposed in the 'eyes', and the game is therefore lost. However, a good percentage of games do go out, and it is satisfying to see the suits growing sideways and joining until four complete suits remain.

# SIX SIXES

*Mystery, Mustery, Mastery*

Lay the first six cards in a row from left to right face-up towards the top centre of the table. Nearer to the bottom of the table lay five fans of six cards each, face-up. Put the remaining cards in a face-down feed-pack. Remove any Aces as they become exposed and place them above the row of six, to be built on in suits. The six cards in the row are built on downwards, overlapping in descending sequence and alternate colours. Any exposed card (in other words the top card) of any fan, or any exposed card in the row, or any building that fits, may be moved to build on the row cards. As a space occurs in the row fill it with the top card of the feed-pack. A space may also be filled by a King exposed at the top of a fan. At any time during the game, but three times only, the top (exposed) card in any fan may be moved to the bottom of that same fan. Build up suits on the Aces. The game ends when the suits are complete, or no further card can be played.

*Went out* 2
      20

---

There is a fascination in the old stories in which three wishes were invited, with the promise that they would be granted. That quickening of the pulse may to a small degree be felt in this game in which three chances of manipulation are offered, the using of which may make or break the game. The 'grantees' of the old stories discovered, often to their cost because they were too impulsive, that it was not the fulfilling of their wishes that proved to be important, but the dire and far-reaching effects. Wisdom in retrospect could not compensate for lack of foresight, unless – ah – that third wish! Now here is a game in which you can, by your foresight, make a judicious choice three times and thus free useful cards which were covered and thus unobtainable, and there is also

Ready to start

In progress

the choice between filling a space with an exposed King or
with a blind card from the feed-pack. The Mystery of the
feed-pack persists for most of the game.

# FORESIGHT

## Mastery

Take the pack and divide it roughly into two halves. Place the first half-pack at the top left and the second half-pack at the bottom left, face-up. With a flat hand gently pat the top pack, drawing the cards away to the right into a row with the numbered edges showing. Do the same with the bottom pack. From the rows take out a total of four cards, each making a gap, and place them side by side in the centre face-up. The separated groups in the rows will now show six exposed cards. (You may need to push the groups apart slightly.) Any of these exposed cards may now be used for building, but one card only may be moved from the groups at any one time. Cover the centre cards by fitting any exposed cards in descending order and alternate colours. Other cards will then be exposed and can be used for building. Any middle card may be used to build on another.

As a space occurs in the four middle places any exposed card may fill the gap, and this card can then be built on or used for building. Any exposed King is removed and placed at the side of the middle cards, two Kings at each side as they appear. These Kings may be built on similarly to the middle cards, and any exposed card and any middle card may be used for such building. Remove any Aces which become exposed, and put them at the top of the table. Build on them in suits in ascending order. Later in the game you may choose a fifth card from anywhere in the top or bottom row to lay in the middle alongside the other four. In doing so you expose another card in the row. Thereafter, any exposed card, but no other, may be used for building or for filling a gap in the middle. The object of the game is to complete the four suits at the top.

*Went out 15*
        *20*

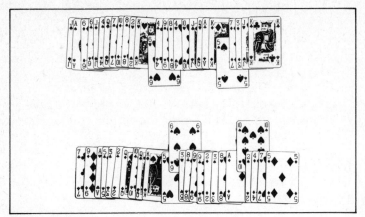

Ready to start

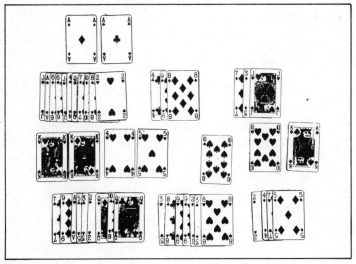

In progress

This is a somewhat untidy game, but one in which a great deal of Mastery is required. The four starting cards should be chosen in such a way that the cards thereby exposed can be used in building, thus freeing further cards which should also be part of your plan for building, leading eventually to the completion of suits. Thus it can be seen that the choice of the four starters requires a deal of foresight. There is no rule as to when a fifth card may be extracted. That is part of the Mastery. There is more freedom of choice in this game than in any other in the book.

Try picking out four cards at random, and see if choosing without foresight has an effect on the outcome of the game.

# MATCH UP

## *Mystery, Mustery*

Place a heap of twelve cards face-up in each of four corners. Put the next card face-up in the centre. Discard the last three cards. Beginning with the top left corner take off the top card of the heap. If it is of the same suit or the same number as the centre card place it on top of that card face-up. If it does not 'match up' place it face-down between its corner heap and the centre card. Repeat this action with the top card at the top right, and so on round the four heaps in rotation. Continue the process, round and round clockwise, matching up with the exposed centre card where possible. Place any picture card as you come to it in the centre, whether it matches the suit or not. The next match up will then be of suit only. When a corner heap is exhausted the process is continued round the other heaps until all are exhausted. Turn up each face-down pack and replace it in the position of the original heap. The

Ready to start

In progress

game is repeated as before. Take the exposed cards in rotation, beginning always with the top left heap, and turn up the face-down packs as before until all the cards are on the centre pile, or until no further card can be played.

*Went out  2*                                    *1 card left  4*
          *20*                                                   *20*

___

When you have counted out three piles of twelve, take the last four cards from the bottom of the remaining pack, rather than counting out another twelve cards.

This is a simple game, demanding little effort except to be alert to the changes of suit or number.


# ACES SAVE

*Mystery, Mustery, Mastery*

Place seven cards from left to right face-up in a row. The remainder of the cards are the feed-pack. Use any exposed card – all the cards will of course be exposed at this stage of the game – to build on any other in alternate colours and descending order. A building may be taken and placed on an exposed card in the order described. As the game progresses, any King, with or without a sequence of followers, may be placed in a space as it occurs through movement of buildings. When no building, or no more building can be done, a further row of seven cards from the feed-pack is laid overlapping the bottom card in each downward row and filling any space. Continue the building and laying seven cards as described above until the feed-pack is exhausted. Each Ace – but only when exposed – is taken out to the side and built on ascending in its own suit. Every time an Ace is removed continue to make as many moves as possible and then, before a further seven cards are laid, choose any one exposed card, remove it, and place it face-down at the side. As you come to the last lay you should have four cards which you can arrange

Ready to start

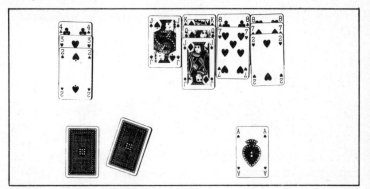

In progress

slightly overlapping. When only three cards are left in the feed-pack pick up the four overlapping face-down cards at the side and put them behind these last three for the last lay. If, when the last three cards are in the hand, less than four Aces have been placed for building, any exposed card or cards may be taken to make up the face-down cards to four, thus completing the seven cards for the last lay.

*Went out 10*
    *20*

Some games have no let-out, but must go inexorably on by sheer Mustery, but here is a game in which a blockage can be released, or at any rate lessened, as each Ace is exposed.

Often a high card can be removed which will come out again conveniently in the last lay for the completion of a suit. Sometimes a low card must be removed as the most judicious move. Again, it is sometimes impossible to make a useful choice, and a card must be removed unwillingly. However, you know that any card so removed will turn up again in the last lay.

# COVER BLACK

*Mystery, Mustery, Mastery*

Place seven cards face-up in a wheel facing a centre space. Put the next seven cards in the space in a face-down heap. The remaining cards are the face-down feed-pack. Exposed cards are built on outwards, overlapping, in descending order and alternate colours. Single cards or buildings in sequence may be moved where appropriate. Remove Aces to the right when they become exposed, and build on them in suits to 10. Begin by building as described, if you can, any of the seven cards in the wheel. When a space occurs in the wheel fill it with the top card of the feed-pack. When no more building can be done, cover black. This means, on every relevant occasion starting with the top spoke of the wheel and moving in a clockwise direction, add to any exposed black card one or more cards until a red card is laid. Do this all round the wheel. Do any more possible building and again, starting from the top, cover black as before.

Pick up the feed-pack and pay it out in threes onto a heap, using any card thus exposed for building as before. If one such card is used, then the next exposed card can also be played if suitable. With every set of three, all possible building should be completed before you cover black. Turn over the used feed-pack again and again and pay out in threes. Build, and cover black, as before. When no further move is possible lay the feed-pack (if any cards remain) face-down at

Ready to start

In progress

the left side. Pick up the seven centre cards and lay them out at the bottom face-up. These are the reserve and may be used for building or for filling any space that occurs. From now on all *exposed* court cards are discarded in the centre. When all the reserve is used up bring back the feed-pack into play for filling any spaces. When, eventually, all the cards are visible face-up, you may at your discretion move into any free space an exposed 10, or a 10 with followers, providing the followers are in descending sequence, as described. The game is completed when all the suits are built up on the Aces.

*Went out 16*
  *20*

---

While some games are neat and orderly, with a set pattern and regular action, this game is irregular after the first lay, and can vary enormously each time in the way it turns out. It is important to remember that before and after each set of three is turned over from the pack, all exposed cards or sequences that can be built should be played, and any space that occurs filled by the card at the top of the feed-pack in your hand. When every possible move is completed, and before the next set of three cards is turned, 'cover black' as explained. The feed-pack is returned again and again to the hand as it becomes used up.

48

# EXCHANGE

*Mastery*

Lay all the court cards, – King, Queen, Jack – in a row
face-up, a suit at a time. The suits can be in any order. Shuffle
the rest of the cards. From the left lay cards in downward
rows below the picture cards face-up and overlapping as
follows: five cards below each King, three cards below each
Queen and two cards below each Jack. Each royal card
collects his own suit by exchange, and places his own in a
heap above him.

*Action 1*   If any card, or cards, are of the same suit as the
court card above them, remove them from the row and place
them in a heap above that court card.

*Action 2*   The remaining cards in the rows are now ex-
changed as follows: a King may exchange from his row either

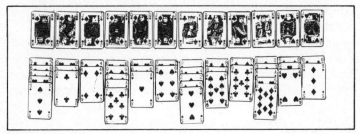

Ready to start

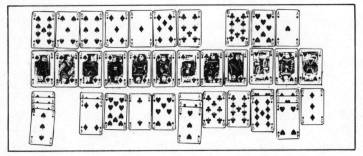

In progress

two, three or five cards at a time for a similar number from another row regardless of suit or suits. He may not exchange a set of four, but may exchange one if he has only one card left in his row. A Queen or a Jack may only exchange the number of cards left in their row, whether they comprise one, two or three cards. As soon as the exchange has been made remove any matching cards to the top heaps as before. Continue the exchanges until each court card has a complete matching set above his head: King five cards, Queen three cards and Jack two cards.

*Went out  6*
       *20*

---

Strangely, it is often the Queen's cards which prove the downfall in this game. The Jack can nearly always exchange his two cards without difficulty. A King has the choice of changing either two, three, or five, which means that he has the freedom of the board. But the Queen is restricted to three, to begin with, and if she is left with three after other exchanges have been made, she may find that there is no other set of three with which to make an exchange. Of course, if she is reduced to two cards her position is simple, and if she has only one there is usually no difficulty at all. If the Jack is left with two cards and all the other cards left are single, since he cannot split his set of two, the game is lost. This game should always go out, if the right moves are made.

# AFTERNOON

## *Mustery, Mastery*

Place the King of Hearts at the top left. Next to him lay the Queen of Hearts, then the Jack of Hearts, from left to right. Continue the row with the other court cards in the same order (King – Queen – Jack). Shuffle the remaining pack. Deal face-up cards below each court card downwards, overlapping, as follows: five cards below each King, three below each Queen and two below each Jack. Exposed cards are now built on in descending order in the same suit, and any building thus made may be removed complete if the first card of the building is of the same suit (and one lower in number) as another exposed card. The building may be placed below, and overlapping, that card. The court cards are not involved in the building, and they remain in place. Each court card collects a certain set of cards. Numbers 1–5 belong to the King of that suit. 6–8 belong to the Queen, and 9 and 10 to the Jack. As each set is completed place it above the appropriate court card. For instance, the set 1–5 of Hearts is put in a heap above the first card laid, in other words, the King of Hearts. If a space occurs under any court card, it may be filled with one card only of its own suit, which is exposed in any other row. The game is won if and when all the cards are in sets above the court cards and none remain below them.

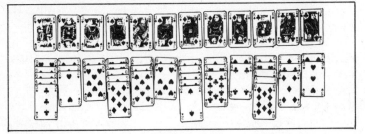

Ready to start

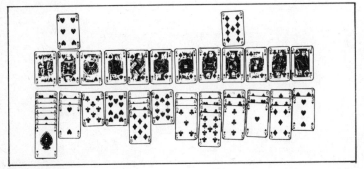

In progress

This game has similar lay-out to Exchange (see page 49), but there the likeness ends, except that in the completed finish the court cards have the same number of cards above them as were placed below them in the first lay. Although this game is mostly Mustery there will be a little choice offered, for example, there may well be a chance to build, say, a 5 on a 6, but that is likely to block the 6–7–8 sequence.

# CHESS-MOVE

*Mastery*

Lay out all the cards in four face-up rows of thirteen, left to right. Take out the Aces and place them at the left of the rows, one before each row. Cards now jump into the spaces as they occur, as follows. Even cards move one place, either up or down or sideways. Odd-numbered cards move one place up, down or sideways, plus one place diagonally. The King may move one place in any direction, straight or diagonally. The Queen may move up, down or along and may jump over any number of cards to a space. The Jack moves only diagonally in any direction and may jump over any number of cards to a space.

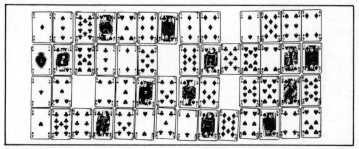

Ready to start

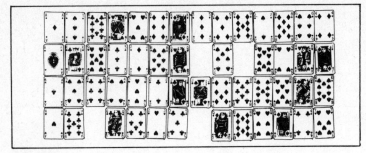

In progress

The game is finished when you have four rows of complete suits, regardless of order.

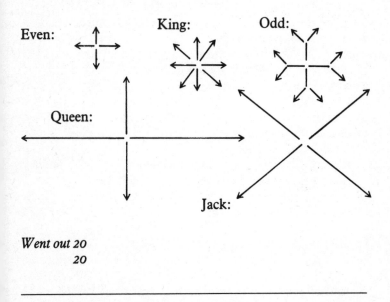

Even:

King:

Odd:

Queen:

Jack:

*Went out 20*
    *20*

It is perhaps best to put an Ace at the beginning of the row which has a predominance of that suit.

The cards move about and about, and by dint of judicious manoeuvring each one slots into place. This is a game in which you can time yourself, and set up a target to beat.

# SEVENS & SIXES

*Mustery, Mastery*

Deal four face-down heaps of seven cards each near the bottom of the table. Put the remaining twenty-four cards in a face-down pack to the right.

*Action 1*    Pick up the first heap of seven cards and hold them face-up. Fan them and place cards as follows. Take out any Kings and put them at the top left in a row left to right. Sets of cards will join this row, as play progresses. Take from your fan any Aces and put them in a downward row on the right. If there are any cards left in your hand which are next to each other in numerical sequence and of alternate colours, lay them in the row placed above, in sequence, each set in a downward overlapping row. If there are no Kings to start with, begin the row with these sequences. If any cards are left in your hand lay them from left to right somewhat below the top row, overlapping. These cards are the free-fan.

*Action 2*    Pick up each of the other three heaps in turn and sort them as in *Action 1*, adding sequences and Kings to the rows and the remainder to the free-fan. Do not build on any of the laid cards at this point.

*Action 3*    Pick up the remaining twenty-four cards and lay them, in four fans of six cards each, at the bottom. Although all the cards are now on view only the exposed cards in the rows and the fans may be used for building, and only one card at a time may be moved. The exception to this rule is the free-fan from which any card may be removed at any time. Build up the top rows in descending order and alternate colours, and build up on the Aces in suits. No building may be moved onto another card. Whenever a King in a fan becomes exposed remove him to the top row. Build on the rows and on the Aces until the suits are complete or no further move can be made.

*Went out 10*
       *20*

When the real action of the game begins all the cards are in view, and all the choices are there to see. Although for most people the actual placing and building of the cards is the interest, for some players it might be possible to play the whole game mentally without moving any cards after the initial lay. It is certainly possible, as the game progresses, to see where necessary cards are blocked in their fans with no hope of release.

Ready to start

In progress

You may be able, in certain circumstances, to build up one suit to, say, the fifth or sixth card, near the beginning of the game, but it is very often wiser to wait, because these cards may be instrumental in releasing necessary cards from the fans, and this will help towards the completion of the game. While our instinct is to complete a suit as soon as possible, it is clear that the completion of all suits is the final aim, and this cannot be achieved while cards are blocked in the fans.

# FRIDAY THE 13th

*Mystery, Mustery, Mastery*

*Action 1* Lay seven cards face-up, left to right. Remove to the left any picture card and any number 10, replacing each with the top card from the pack regardless of its denomination. Sweep the seven cards to the right. Lay seven more cards and repeat the process. Continue to do this until the pack is finished. Towards the end, only those cards are removed that can be replaced by cards in the hand; if there are seven cards or less sweep them to the right without removing any.

*Action 2* Pick up the cards on the right, turn them over, shuffle them and repeat *Action 1*.

*Action 3* Pick up, turn over and shuffle the cards on the right, then lay them face-up as follows: near the top left lay a row of seven cards downwards overlapping; to the right of that a similar row, but of five cards; then a row of three cards, then one card, then three, five, seven, five, three, one and so on, until all the cards in the hand are laid.

*Action 4* Remove any Aces to the bottom as they become exposed and build up the suits on them when you are able. Build downwards on exposed cards as follows: one (exposed) card only may be moved at a time either onto a card of the next highest denomination and of alternate colour, or to build up the suits on the Aces. When a space occurs in the rows it may be filled by any exposed card. If and when the cards are all built up in the suits any remaining picture card is left in place on the table and incorporated in the laying of the next cards.

*Action 5* Pick up the cards on the left which were removed in *Actions 1 and 2*, and lay them as in *Action 3*, but in rows of five, three, one, three, four, according to the number of cards left. Continue as in *Action 4* moving one card at a time and building onto the suits at the bottom until they are complete or until no further moves can be made.

Ready to start

In progress

*Went out 13*
20

This game is in two parts, and if the first part goes out there is still the further hurdle to be negotiated in *Action 5*. If the fifth action goes out you have a double satisfaction.

The object of the first action is to eliminate the 10s and court cards. There are points for and against any of the high cards being left in the playing pack for *Action 3*. They can be awkward, and may actually block play, but they also cause the laying of an extra row, even if it consists of one card only, and this can be very useful for creating a space.

# THREE TRIES

## *Mystery, Mustery*

*Action 1 (part 1)*   Lay six cards in a row from left to right face-up. The remaining cards are the face-down feed-pack. Build on any exposed card – they will all be exposed at this stage of the game, of course – in downward sequence and in alternate colours overlapping. You may use any exposed card to build, and sequences may be removed and added below a fitting exposed card. As a space occurs fill it with the top card of the feed-pack. Remove Aces as they become exposed and place them to the right and build on them in upward sequence in suits. Any exposed King is removed and placed to the left of the original row of cards, and built on downwards as indicated, that is, by alternate number and colour. When no further building can be done pick up all the face-up cards in order from the left, except the suits built on the Aces. (Begin with the Kings and their followers.) Place all these picked-up cards in a pack at the top face-down.

*Action 1 (part 2)*   Pick up the bottom pack and begin again with a row of six cards. Keep repeating *part 1*, adding the picked-up cards to the top pack, until no more cards remain in the bottom pack.

*Action 2*   Pick up the top pack and lay six cards downwards overlapping, face-up, at the left. To the right of that row lay another similar six cards, and continue with rows of six until all the cards are laid. Build up as before any exposed card or sequence, also building up the suits on the right. Kings and their sequences, if any, are placed at the left and built on as before. Any suitable exposed card in the sequence below a King may be moved to build up the suit on an Ace.

*Action 2 (part 2)* When no further move is possible pick up the cards from the left as before but leaving Kings and their followers. Repeat *Action 1*.

These three actions only are allowed. The game finishes when all four suits are complete, or no further move is possible.

Ready to start

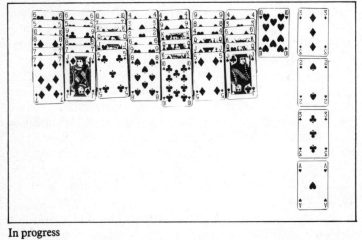

In progress

*Went out 16*     *Went out in 3 tries 11*     *Went out in 2 tries 5*
20                  20                  20

This game varies tremendously from one go to another. Sometimes it all but goes out in the first try, sometimes in the second it goes out. It nearly always goes out by the third, but occasionally it will not go out. I have never found it go out in one try only, but it is quite possible for it to do so.

If the game proceeds to *Action 3*, it will be seen that if a situation develops where no further building can be done, and the feed-pack is not exhausted, the game will not go out, as the picked-up cards in *Action 3* cannot be used again, and therefore the suits cannot be completed.


# THE FIVES

*Mystery, Mustery, Mastery*


*Action 1 (part 1)*   Lay five cards in a row left to right face-up. Lay a similar row of five below and overlapping the first row, and continue until five rows of five cards have been laid. Put the rest of the pack face-down at the bottom of the table. Build on any exposed card with a card of the next lower number and alternate colour, which is removed for this purpose from any of the four other rows together with all the cards that lie below it, whatever their denomination. Remove exposed Aces to the right and exposed Kings to the left. Continue to build on the exposed cards as described. Build on Aces upwards in suits and on Kings downwards, overlapping, in descending order and alternate colours. A building comprising a number of cards may be moved to a King's row provided they are in sequence. Any exposed card in a King's row may be used to build up the suit on the Ace. The Kings' rows and the Aces' heaps are not picked up with the other cards in the following actions.

*Action 1 (part 2)*   When no further building can be done pick up the rows of cards in order from the left, and put them in a face-up heap at the top. Repeat *part 1* with the other half of the pack, laying the last two cards below as a reserve. Use these two cards also to build if they fit. When all possible building as in *part 1* is finished, pick up the cards in order as before. Pick up the reserve cards if they have not been used, and add them to the top pack. Place the second pack on top of the first, face-up.

*Action 2* Pick up and turn over the pack. Lay five cards downwards overlapping, face-up. Lay four more similar rows to the right of the first. Repeat the building as in *Action 1* *(part 1)* and then pick up the cards and remove them as before. Lay out the remainder of the pack similarly, build, then remove, and place on top of the first pack.

Ready to start

In progress

*Action 3*  As *Action 1*.
*Action 4*  As *Action 2*.
*Action 5*  As *Action 1*. This completes the game.

| *Went out 18* | *In 2 Actions*  1 | *In 4 Actions*  4 |
| 20 | 20 | 20 |

| *In 1 Action*  0 | *In 3 Actions*  4 | *In 5 Actions*  9 |
| 20 | 20 | 20 |

There are three different methods of building in this game:
1) Building upwards in suits on the Aces.
2) Building in descending order and alternate colour on the Kings, overlapping downwards.
3) Moving a number of unrelated cards together onto a card in another row.

It is not often that this game fails to go out, but it can take a varying number of actions from *1* to *5*. There is something very satisfying in being able to move a card into place even though it is not exposed. Sometimes a choice must be made if two of the same number and colour are available for play. Then the cards which would become exposed by the move must be considered. It is as well to build downwards on the Kings as far as possible, even if you break up a building in the rows to do so. Thus, for example, if there is a downward row from red 10 to black 3, it is wise to remove the black 7 and followers in sequence to build on a King's suit with an exposed red 8. It is a good idea to have some small counters at one side; even matches will do. At the beginning of each lay, move a counter across, to indicate which lay it is.

# RECOVERY

## Mystery, Mustery, Mastery

Deal ten cards into a large inward-facing semi-circle face-up.

Deal ten more cards onto the first ten, face-up, overlapping. Do this twice more. The remaining cards are the feed-pack.

Use any exposed card to build on any other in descending order and alternate colours. Buildings thus made may be used to build on any exposed card in the same order. Remove any exposed Aces to the central space and build on them in suits in ascending order. When no further building can be done, pick up the feed-pack face-down and deal the cards in threes onto a heap, using the exposed card for building as before, and using any other suitable card that becomes exposed. When a space occurs in the semi-circle, fill it with the top face-down card of the feed-pack. The discard heap is picked up, turned over and used again and again. When the feed-pack is used up, any space in the semi-circle can be filled by any exposed King or a King with followers in sequence.

The game has 'gone out' if all the suits are completed.

*Went out 13*
  *20*

---

You can improve your chances of 'succeeding' in this game by shrewdly delaying the filling of gaps in the semi-circle. There is no rule as to when you should fill a gap, and you can run through the feed-pack as many times as you like before you do so. Since the order of the cards in the feed-pack changes every time a card is removed, you can wait until such a change is necessary before taking off a card to fill a gap. This strategy will nearly always lead to a satisfactory conclusion.

Ready to start

In progress

# INDEX

| Page | Title of game | Mystery, Mustery or Mastery (see below) | Space needed | (x) Can be played with 1 hand | Went out (out of 20) |
|------|---------------|------------------------------------------|--------------|-------------------------------|----------------------|
| 9 | Smoke | a b c | Medium | x | 8 times |
| 10 | Move up | a b c | Small | x | 8 times |
| 12 | Eight across | a c | Small | x | 0 times |
| 13 | Jack be nimble | a b | Small | x | 0 times |
| 15 | As you like | a c | Medium | | 10 times |
| 17 | Six fives | a b c | Medium | x | 10 times |
| 19 | Republic | c | Medium | | 9 times |
| 21 | Tower of London | a b c | Large | x | 7 times |
| 24 | Equality | a b | Small | x | 1 time |
| 25 | Boxing Day | a b c | Large | | 12 times |
| 28 | Tournament | a c | Large | | 18 times |
| 30 | Absorption | a c | Medium | x | 5 times |
| 31 | Teaser | c | Large | x | 20 times |
| 33 | Fanny | a b c | Large | | 15 times |
| 35 | Seek your own | a b | Small | | 2 times |
| 36 | Rapide or 12 into 4 | a c | Small | x | 0 times |
| 38 | Long nose | a b | Medium | | 7 times |
| 40 | Six sixes | a b c | Medium | | 2 times |
| 42 | Foresight | c | Large | x | 15 times |
| 44 | Match up | a b | Small | x | 2 times |
| 45 | Aces save | a b c | Medium | | 10 times |
| 47 | Cover black | a b c | Medium | | 16 times |
| 49 | Exchange | c | Large | | 6 times |
| 50 | Afternoon | b c | Large | x | 8 times |
| 52 | Chess-move | c | Large | x | 20 times |
| 54 | Sevens & Sixes | b c | Large | | 10 times |
| 56 | Friday the 13th | a b c | Large | x | 13 times |
| 58 | Three tries | a b | Medium | x | 16 times |
| 60 | The fives | a b c | Medium | | 18 times |
| 62 | Recovery | a b c | Large | x | 13 times |

*a – Mystery  b – Mustery  c – Mastery*